The Inept Society?

Incompetence in America

The Inept Society?

Jess Browning

BRONCO ePUBLISHING

Bainbridge Island, Washington

The Inept Society?

Bronco ePublishing, LLC
Bainbridge Island, Washington

Incompetence in America: The Inept Society?

ISBN-13: 978-1722080495
ISBN-10: 1722080493

Copyright © 2018 by Jess Browning,

First published 2018.

Most of the sources used in this book are copyrighted with some being in the public domain. The use of extracts from sources has been in a transformative manner different from their original intended use. Where possible, permission has been requested and given for use of excerpts. In cases where it has been impossible to contact the source, excerpts have been used under the doctrine of "fair use". Permission has been obtained for images used. Any mistakes, misrepresentations, or errors of omission that may occur are regretted. None of the sources mentioned have endorsed this work in anyway. If you are the copyright holder of a source used and disagree with its use, contact www.broncoepublishing.com.

Some copyright material referenced is under terms of the GNU Free Documentation License http://en.wikipedia.org/wiki/GNU_Free_Documentation_License.

For Creative Commons Licenses see their websites http://creativecommons.org/licenses/by-sa/2.0/deed.en and http://creativecommons.org/licenses/by-sa/3.0/

Inept America Competence Society Communication Worst Ability

Incompetence in America

The Inept Society?

8

Books in Print

Black & White Non-fiction
Technology, the Economy & Jobs: A Historical Perspective
Ancient European Ancestors (A Grey Tones Edition)
Brownings in England (A Grey Tones Edition)
Captain John Browning (A Grey Tones Edition)
Jess and his Family: Genealogy and History (Grey Tones Edition)
Global Logistics and Trade: Intermodal Transport
The Innovation Process: Educating and Teaching
Respect for Labor
The Deceitful and Insidious Web
Seattle to England by Surface Transport

Books Edited
King Arthur & Modred: A Young King in Waiting
King Arthur & Sir Balin: A Knight with Two Swords
King Arthur & Pellianore: A Father of Knights
King Arthur & Sir Gawaine: Their Adventures
King Arthur & Rome: Ambassadors Demand Tribute
King Arthur & Lancelot: Their Fights & Affairs
King Arthur & **Gareth***: The Kitchen Boy*
King Arthur & Tristram: The Fighter
King Arthur & Knights: Lovers and Fighters
King Arthur & Sir Tristram & Sir Lancelot
King Arthur & Sir Lancelot
King Arthur & Sir Lancelot
King Arthur & Sir Lancelot
King Arthur & Sir Lancelot & Sir Percival

King Arthur & Sir Gawaine
King Arthur & Queen's Joy
King Arthur & Sir Galahad
King Arthur & Sir Lancelot & Guinevere
King Arthur & Gawaine
King Arthur & Mordred
Black & White Historical Fiction: Short Stories
The Nomads: Their Migration Experiences
The Anglos: Their Pleasures and Travails
Southwest England: Life and Times 1390 to 1430 AD
Captain John: From England to Virginia
Francis: Plantation Owner, Merchant & Tobacco Farmer
Caleb: The Frontier Man
Jeb: His Family and History
William T.: A Man to Look up to
China: 1979
The Families: A Compendium of Stories
Vicki: A Mystery
King Edward the Second of England
Black & White Collected Short Stories
Anatolia to Britain: A Trilogy
America's Frontier: Virginia to California
Compendium of Short Stories: From Eurasia to Seattle
The Life and Times of King Arthur: A Compendium
Black & White Biographies
Life and Times of Jess Sr.
Life and Times of Anna Love.
Jess Jr.: A DIY Guy
Cec and Caroline: A Wonderful Life!

Vicki: A Cheerleader
Some Swank Descendants
Some Perdue Descendants
Color Non-fiction
Ancient European Ancestors: DNA, Archeological, Historical & Linguistic Evidence
Browning's in England: Records of where, when & how they lived
Captain John Browning: A Family History in England & Virginia from 1255 to 1799 AD
Jess and his Family: Genealogy and History

The Inept Society?

Dedication

This book is dedicated to all who have endured the time spent by the author on its research, writing, editing and publication.

It is especially dedicated to my wife Vicki, my daughters Carrie, Alexa, Nanci and Susan as well as to grandchildren, sisters, relatives, ancestors and friends.

The book is also dedicated to the referenced sources noted which were of great help in providing a work that is hoped to be of educational value to the broader community. The inclusion of these sources adds immensely to the story presented in a critical manner and the brief nature of its inclusion has no reflection on its value.

Specific citations are given when information is available and when not available credit is given based on the source.

Most of the characters in this book are fictional and their names do not reflect real people.

The picture on the cover is from the publishing house, CreateSpace.com.

Contents

The Inept Society?

Introduction

This story has a mystery novel wrapped into it to make it more interesting and informative. The novel begins by describing the characters in Chapter 2. The main character, Henry, is one of those people who has to communicate with people in many organizations.

Many of us have had trouble in dealing with an issue with some organization over the telephone. We have to wait as an automated voice tells us what we need to do next in making a call. This is after telling us to push a button on our phone to let them know in what language we want to communicate. Then we may be told to choose from a menu, telling us what button to push. We are then often advised that the wait time is going to be a number of minutes. Sometimes, the computer generated voice tell us that "due to the call volume" we may need to call back at another time. Often they just tell us to leave a message.

This process is all very troublesome not to mention that it is time consuming and very expensive for us. Then, when we do get a real voice on the line, the challenge begins.

This is especially true of the Medical and Drug industries. The opioid crisis is one example of what is going on. The Food and Drug Administration (FDA) seems to be over acting in dealing with the problem. The average addiction threshold for adults is about 75 milligrams a day of an opioid such as hydrocodone or oxycodone.

The FDA has told prescription writers in the medical facilities to limit the amount dispensed at pharmacies as much as possible. This requires that doctors try to limit the intake of opioids by prescribing a limited amount per day for a given period of usually about a month. This means that a user has to keep track of their intake and order a renewal of the pain drug a few days to a week ahead of time.

In 2010, the US government began cracking down on pharmacists and doctors who were over-prescribing opioid painkillers. An unintended consequence of this was that those addicted to prescription opiates turned to heroin, a significantly more potent but cheaper opioid, as a substitute.

Also in 2010, the Controlled Substances Act was amended with the Secure and Responsible Drug Disposal Act, which allows pharmacies to accept controlled substances from households or long-term care facilities in their drug disposal programs or "take-back" programs. All of the above substances, and more, are under government control as specified in the Controlled Substances Act (CSA).

It is a statute establishing federal U.S. Drug policy, which regulates the manufacture, importation, possession, use, and distribution of certain substances. It was passed by the 91st United States Congress as Title II of the Comprehensive Drug Abuse Prevention and Control Act of 1970 and signed into law by the President. It is overseen by the Health and Human Service Resources (HSR) and is enforced by the Federal Trade Commission (FTC).[1]

The Food and Drug Administration logo was formed on June 30, 1906. It is well over one hundred years old. The FDA is one of its departments. The FDA is responsible for protecting and promoting public health through the control and supervision of food safety, tobacco products, dietary supplements, prescription and over-the-counter pharmaceutical drugs (medications), medical devices, vaccines, biopharmaceuticals, blood transfusions, electromagnetic radiation emitting devices, cosmetics, animal foods & feed and veterinary products. As of 2017, threeforths of the FDA budget, approximately $700 million, is funded by the pharmaceutical companies as a result of the Prescription Drug User Fee Act.[2]

On January 12, 2018, the Federal Trade Commission and the FDA sent out warning letters to eleven marketers and distributors of opioid cessation products. The recipients of the letters were to reply to the FDA in 15 days of the action taken on their part. In general the FDA also stated that they should take prompt action to correct the violations cited and that failure to promptly correct the violations may result in legal action without further notice, including, without limitation, seizure and/or injunction. It is assumed that similar letters were sent out to various doctors in hospital and clinics around the country earlier in about 2016.[3]

Early in 2017, the Seattle Times reported that the FDA was telling everyone involved in prescribing medicine to reduce the consumption of opioids. Henry and the FBI were likely involved in this operation to reduce drug use.

In control of the opioid epidemic, doctors are required to keep the addiction threshold at a very low level in which the dosage rate is well below the addiction rate.

Most organizations today are doing very well economically and people are hired to improve the organization's bottom-line. In doing so, people are trained to pacify the caller who usually has a problem and is angry. Many times the caller has a problem, that may deal with money, a guarantee, a medical issue, etc. and the caller wants to resolve the issue. Since the person on the organization's phone knows that callers, taken together, affect the organization's bottom-line, they are trained to deal with a problem caller in a way that minimizes cost to the organization and in many cases, the caller is pleased with the conversation but has not been able to resolve the problem. Many times they are passed off to another person who is also well trained in avoiding issues that will affect the organization monetarily.

It seems like each company one calls uses different robotic software to address the callers. Today the author called a company to dispute a bill and went through much of the scenario presented in the example above but with a new twist. He had to key in on the telephone keypad his the six digits of his birthdate by day, month and year then the robotic voice asked him to verify the information and he had to do it again. Then the robotic voice ask him to pronounce his full name and date of birth and then to verify it again. He was also ask to enter on the telephone key board his account number and verify it. Once he was in contact with the real person, he was asked the same information again.

The above examples are typical of today's communications between customers and organizations. In addition, it is understood that a lot has to do with legalities. There are many other examples that talk about how organizations deal with people and each other in a way that may affect their balance sheet in a negative way.

It may appear that people in organizations have a lack of skill or ability but that may not be the case. They may be doing their job the way their organization wants it done.

In the story, Henry seems to understand all this. He knows that his old childhood friend who works for the CIA has become a criminal and possibly a murderer. He was getting drugs, especially the opiate variety, from an orderly who worked in a medical center. Henry's old friend whose name was Frank was repackaging the stolen drugs after modifying them which made some of the drugs very dangerous.

The opioids were in greater supply due to the restriction policies of the FDA.

Henry had come to Seattle at the request of Frank but, as he learned more about what was going on, he wanted no part of it. Henry found that people, including Frank, had serious character flaws that hindered his investigations .

Incompetence in America

The Inept Society?

Chapter 1: Terminology

There are a number of terms that need to be understood prior to proceeding with the story. It includes the words "adept, inept, incompetence, opioids, organization, and society. It is mainly about the drugs as addressed in this story but, the terms apply to the larger society in general."

Adept[4]

An adept person is identified as having attained a specific level of knowledge, skill, or aptitude in doctrines relevant to a particular author or organization.

Organizations may also operate illegally in the case of secret societies, criminal organizations and resistance movements but are not discussed here.

Inept[5]

An inept person is one who is not able to do something; the person is not proficient or displays incompetence. It is a person who is unfit or unsuitable. Inept is a word borrowed from the French language by the English.

Incompetence[6]

Incompetence is a person's inability to perform. It is a lack of competence or a case of ineptitude.

Aspects of incompetence include:

- *Administrative incompetence* is a dysfunctional administrative behavior that hinders attainment of organization goals.
- *Incompetence in law* describes a person not of sound mind who is mentally impaired and unable to make decisions for himself or herself.
- *Military incompetence* is failure of members of the military.
- *Social ineptitude is* another aspect of incompetence.

Opioids[7]

The opioid epidemic or opioid crisis is the rapid increase in the use of prescription and non-prescription opioid drugs in the United States and Canada beginning in the late 1990s and has continued throughout the following two decades.

Opioids are a diverse class of moderately strong painkillers, including oxycodone, commonly sold under the trade names OxyContin and Percocet. Opioids include hydrocodone, and a very strong painkiller, fentanyl, which is synthesized to resemble other opiates such as opium-derived morphine and heroin.

Organization[8]

An organization is an entity comprising multiple people, such as an institution or an association, that has a collective goal and is linked to an external environment. There are a variety of legal types of organizations, including corporations, governments, non-governmental, political, international, armed forces, charities, non-profits, partnerships, cooperatives, and educational institutions.

Society[9]

A society is a group of individuals involved in social interaction or is a large social group sharing the same geographical or social territory, typically subject to the same political authority and dominant cultural expectations.

Societies are characterized by patterns of relationships (social relations) between individuals who share a distinctive culture and institutions; a given society may be described as the sum total of such relationships among its constituent of members.

A society may enable its members to benefit in ways that would not otherwise be possible on an individual basis; both individual and social (common) benefits can thus be distinguished, or in many cases found to overlap.

A society may also consist of like-minded people governed by their own norms and values within a dominant, larger society. More broadly a society may be illustrated as an economic, social, industrial or cultural infrastructure, made up of a varied collection of individuals.

All of these concepts *adept, inept, incompetence, opioids, organization, and society* are important considerations not only to what goes on in this book but also in everyday life.

I think that each of us can relate to the individual concepts. For example the first three *adept, inept and incompetence* are closely related. We may be adept at something if we want to but if we decide not to we may be considered inept. A person looking on from the outside who is not aware of our capabilities may say. "That person is incompetent".

Henry's old friend Frank says that he is an amoral person, which means he is neither moral nor immoral. This means that he is moving to a different beat than Henry who accepts the concepts of one being adept, inept or incompetent.

An amoral person can easily move into crime like Frank has done. He had been investigating the looseness in the drug industry on behalf of the CIA and in his search for problems in the industry, his philosophy of being amoral allowed him to consider how much money could be made by teaming up with someone with access to medications.

Frank's amoral philosophy allowed him through his CIA investigation put him in contact with an orderly at a medical center, which gave him the connection that he needed.

Incompetence in America

The Inept Society?

34

Chapter 2: Characters

The Characters: The story begins with the characters.

Henry James is a descendant of Frank James, brother of Jesse James who were both outlaws and basic members of the James Gang that terrorized Western Missouri and Eastern Kansas with bank and train robberies. Many people loved them however viewing them as Robin Hood types that robbed from the rich and gave to the poor. Even though his ancestors were outlaws, they and their descendants were viewed as being good natured people.

Henry is the FBI investigator that is following the opioid crisis closely. Years of dealing with incompetence with other people in his investigations has left Henry somewhat cynical.

He has several aliases such as Gene Whilde and is one of the few characters in the story who is not incompetent or mentally off-balance. Another name that he used somewhat was Jack Alberson. Although, he has various aliases, his surname name is not given in the story except by his former mentor and childhood friend, who refers to him as Henry James.

Henry has had to communicate with many different people in various organizations and has learned to exploit society's incompetence as described in Chapter 1 in order to aid his investigations.

He seems to be one of very few people who can do anything well, although he remarks that most people who get nowhere is because of their ineptitude.

Frank is Henry's former mentor and fellow agent who Henry at first thought was dead. But his death was faked and Henry was surprised to find that his former friend was not only consuming drugs but was also dealing in them.

Agent Browne is an FBI Agent and leader as well as Henry's boss in the Agency. By Browne's own admission, he sometimes becomes a bit overbearing and has serious difficulty controlling his anger. Although often irrational and angry, he has a genuine desire to uphold the law and withhold his anger.

He is a leader since he is known to be depended on in following the law. However he often become angry because of believing that his work was being interfered with. His overreaction make him appear less than rational but to Henry's surprise, he is not lacking in skills as an FBI Agent.

Georgia Hallister is a pretty and voluptuous showgirl who suffers from inappropriate sexual response with men that she views as strong and overpowering; she is an object of Henry's lust, companionship and information.

William Baker, **MD** or Doc has hobbies that are varied in the drug and medical field. For example, he loved to experiment with various drugs on body parts injecting them with a drug such as women breasts and men's penis that caused them to become erect.

Hugh Clinton is an ex-legal assistant who visited the prison that Henry was incarcerated in hopes of getting him out or getting more information on the case. Unfortunately, he found himself, supposedly due to no fault of his own, in jail.

PA is a Personal Assistant who does all the things needed that at the primary individual cannot do or does not want to do because of the way they were brought up or due to time constraints. The formal definition is that a personal assistant is also referred to as personal aide (PA). It describes a person who assists another person with his or her daily business or personal tasks.

Orderly is this book is the one working in the medical facility that has access to the medications. It is also an attendant in a hospital responsible for the nonmedical care of patients and the maintenance of order and cleanliness. It is usually a hospital attendant whose job consists of assisting medical and nursing staff with various nursing and medical interventions.[10] In most cases, they have access to drugs and medicine depending on the medical facility.

First Un-Named Friend of Frank is who was with Frank when he was hit by the truck.

Second Un-Named Friend is who helped the first friend move Frank from the accident scene.

The Inept Society?

Chapter 3: In Seattle

This story tells of a Henry working for an unnamed secret agency with a variety of identities within various law enforcement agencies but primarily the FBI.

At the beginning of the story Henry and Frank get drunk together and talk of the good times they have had. It is several months earlier in LA where they are both in town for business. Frank has a room in the Marriott Hotel in Torrance and Henry has a room in the Holiday Hotel across Hawthorne Boulevard.

After he arrived and got checked into the hotel he went across the boulevard to see Frank who knew he was coming and left a message that he was in the bar. It was where Frank and Henry spent most of their time together.

Later Henry James comes to Seattle seeking Frank who during their sessions in the bar has offered him a CIA type job.

Upon arrival in Seattle, Henry discovers that Frank was killed just hours earlier by a speeding truck while crossing the street. Henry attends Frank's funeral, where he meets his FBI superior, Agent Browne, who says Frank is a criminal and suggests Henry leave Seattle to avoid prosecution of Frank's murder or of suffering the same fate that Frank suffered.

Henry reminds Browne that he is a deep undercover American agent hired by the U. S. Trade Commission to destroy any possibilities of the United States drug industry expanding. More specifically to stop the Opioid Crisis. Moreover, if Frank knows anything about the drug trade, he needs to talk with him.

In his investigation, Henry is hindered by the fact that practically everyone he meets or talks with has a serious character flaw and or a hang-up that hinders his investigations very much.

Henry seems to be facing many difficulties. Another ongoing problem is his inability to acquire or hang onto a decent pair of pants, since all seem to be made of some inferior Chinese material. Apparently, Henry bought some clothes in China and the pants along with the other clothes were guaranteed for a year but the pants were failing, coming apart at the seams, after only a month.

If that was not enough, a Seattle Police Detective approaches Henry and tells him that he must remain in town since he is a suspect in Frank's murder.

Henry accepted this as an opportunity to clear his friend's name and it gives him more time to continue his investigation. Being with the FBI, he can probably leave whenever he wants but he decides to remain in Seattle.

He receives information from a friend of Frank's who tells Henry that he, along with another friend, carried Frank to the side of the street after the accident. The friends never came forward after that but, as we will see later, The Seattle Police Department would want to talk with them.

Before dying, the friend said that Frank wanted him and the second guy to take care of Henry and Georgia Hallister, Frank's actress girlfriend. Unfortunately, neither friend stepped forward to help. It is not clear what Frank was thinking, especially since he considered himself an amoral person.

Incompetence in America

Chapter 4: Investigation of Drugs & Murder

In the course of his investigations for both drugs and murder, Henry did this investigation under his alias of Gene Whilde

He had trouble in dealing with an opioid issue with a hospital over the telephone. First he had to wait as an automated voice told him what next in making the call. This is after telling us to push a button on our phone to let them know in what language to communicate. Then he was told to choose from a menu, telling him what button to push.

He was then advised that the wait time was going to be about seven minutes and was advised to leave a message where someone could call him back. In calling another medical facility, the computer-generated voice told him that "due to the call volume" they would need to call back at another time and told him to leave a message with name and phone number.

Examples of incompetence affecting Agent Gene were:

1. Incomplete records: When he was able to make contact with a person and ask for information on drug tests, it was sent to him but was missing data and was not complete.
2. Contradiction with other documents that are simply false such as death certificates. He was amazed that King County had already issued a death Certificate on Frank.
3. He was also amazed that FBI agents would obliterate all evidence by walking casually through a crime scene.
4. Inaccurate local guides and transport. Getting around Seattle was not easy despite its vast array of transportation services. When he was able to get a taxi for example, he would be very upset that the driver could not communicate with him in English.
5. He found that it was often the case that people could not work the basic equipment they were paid to use.

Many of the people that Gene was in contact with seemed to be incompetent to him but their ineptness may have been more to a lack of training than lack of ability.

ineptness may have been more to a lack of training than lack of ability.

The Inept Society?

Chapter 5: Georgia

Henry hoping to gather more information on Frank, he goes to see Georgia at her theatre. He knocks on her stage door and she opens it immediately. He looks her up and down and in his own mind and thinks that she is one of the most beautiful women he has ever seen.

He estimates her to be about 5 feet seven inches tall, she has long black hair that cascades down over her shoulders and her blue eyes are intense. Her body is smooth and firm. He estimated her weight at about 115 pounds, her legs taper in a seductive way from her small feet up to her thighs. Her waist is small and her ample breasts are two sooth orbs that reveal hard nipples that jiggle with movement beneath her gown. Initially, Henry believes Georgia to be a figment of his imagination, but realizes that he doesn't have that great an imagination, she is real.

To Georgia, Henry looked like a Greek God; tall, about six foot four inches with a hard, bronze body and he weighed about 220 pounds. He had blue-grey eyes and blond curly hair. At once, she felt excitement flooding through her body and a hot sensation in her vagina. She knew that she was ovulating. She immediately thought of Frank whom she often loved and had intercourse, but the feeling were there and she was full of desire.

They talk somewhat suggestively: Henry says, "It looks like I came at a good time. I know that we could have a good time together." And he moves toward her. She backs up and says, "I'm sure we could have a great time together, but I still have to think of Frank. He said, "Frank bought the farm and I don't think he would mind."

She suggests in passing that Frank's death may not have been accidental and he may still be around. She says, "I have hope that he is still alive, since I do love him very much. As far as you go, I could be with you for a good time since you do arouse my feelings, but at this time I say definitely no!"

Henry manages to convince her to go out on an exploratory date by saying, I know you and

Frank were lovers but he is not with us anymore and it wouldn't hurt anyone if we spent some time getting to know each other." "She says, "I know you are right and you look trust-worthy, so yes I agree that it would be ok."

Unfortunately, Henry fails to turn up because he is arrested by the Seattle Police on suspension of murdering Frank but is released later, after he proved to them that he was not yet in the area when the murder occurred.

Before the end of the book, however, Henry tells Browne that he has an unbeliveable hot date, so hot that it could incapacitate the partner; however, he still managed to convince her to go on another date.

Unfortunately, Georgia is showing a desire to do a good job in her affair with Henry and worries herself so much that it makes her a bad sexual performer. She is overwhelmed by what she envisions to be a large Greek God but her desire does not stop her from trying. She still loves Frank but is willing to experience love with Henry who says, "Georgia, this is a natural act for two people who are willing. I know you still have feeling for Frank but he would like to see you happy." He enters her and she almost panics. She thinks, "He is so large and hard. I can't do this."

After their attempt at love making, she then accompanies Henry to question Frank's Personnel Assistant in the apartment building they lived in. A personal assistant is also referred to as personal aide (PA) and it describes a person who assists another person with their daily business or personal tasks. Frank's PA claims that Frank was killed immediately and could not have given any instructions to his friends before dying.

The PA also states that Frank's body was not moved out of the street only by his friend, but that his friend was helped by another person.

Henry berates the PA for not being more forthcoming with the FBI about what he knows being concerned for his family's safety. Henry says, "What were you thinking about when you were first interviewed by the FBI. It is illegal to hold back information which can carry a stiff penalty." The PA indignantly tells Henry not to involve him and says, "I know that I was in the wrong but I have my family to think of. Please do not pursue this anymore with me. I can be killed not to mention my family members."

Shortly afterwards, the FBI is searching Georgia's flat for evidence. They find and confiscate her forged passport and she is detained. Georgia says, "Henry my passport is not legal and if it is inspected very closely, the FBI will find that it is false and they will deport me."

After Georgia tells Henry that she is an illegal alien and will be deported from the U. S. if discovered, she says, "I still care for Frank, but I can't get you out of my mind. Please don't give up on me and give me another chance. I just think that I am intimidated by your size and the fact that we haven't performed together much."

Henry says, "I understand Georgia and know of your feelings for your dead lover, but lets keep each other in our thoughts and whenever we have the chance, let's do it again."

Incompetence in America

The Inept Society?

58

Chapter 6: The Doctor

Henry visits Frank's "medical adviser", Doc, who was in the middle of one of his sordid hobbies involving the effect of drugs on body parts. When Henry came to visit, Doc was in the process of injecting a drug into cadaver bodies that he kept around for such purposes. The cadavers had little odor since they were well treated with a formaldehyde solution.

Doc thought, "Shit, I was just in the middle of injecting a dead woman's breasts and a dead man's penis that would hopefully cause the nipples and penis to become erect. Then I planned to remove the penis and insert it in the dead woman's vagina."

Fortunately, Doc stopped what he was doing and gave attention to Henry's questioning. The doctor said, "I arrived at the accident after Frank was dead, and only one man, the PA, was present.

Later, the PA secretly offers Henry more information but is murdered before their arranged meeting. The PA's worse fear had come true. Some murderer went after him and he was killed, although his family was ok.

A young boy recognized Henry as having argued with the PA earlier and points this out to the gathering by-standers, who had followed Henry to the doctor's office. The youngster said aloud to the by-standers, "It must have been him who did the murder since I later saw him arguing with the other fellow. So it must be him." The on-lookers became hostile, and then mob-like going after Henry."

Escaping from the mob, Henry returns to the hotel, and a cab whisks him away to another investigation. In Henry's investigation he works to track down the unknown stalker and has the uneasy feeling that it is Frank who is listed on a death certificate but could still be alive living under an alias.

Henry has trouble accepting the fact that Frank's PA had been murdered. He wonders, "There sure seems to be a lot of murders here in town. First it was Frank getting hit by a truck and now his Personnel Assistant is dead. What is this world coming to? I'm going have to pick up the pace or it will be me that bites the dust."

Henry goes to visit the Los Angeles Police Department detective who is in charge of Frank's murder to see what information might be available. It is a long taxi ride from the Holiday Inn in Torrance to Central Los Angeles, but to Henry time is of the essence and he does not want to waste time dealing with a telephone robot.

The detective is amiable and is easy to tall with. They being with a lot of small talk, about where they grew up, how they entered law enforcement and some of their Vietnam experiences.

He finds out some of the information that Browne gives him the next day about Frank's clandestine activities and about his orderly connection. Henry give thought to what he has learned, "I'm beginning to think that Frank may no longer be the nice guy I used to know. It seems that he is working crookedly in areas that he is supposed to be controlling. Having a close connection with an orderly in a medical facility is not a good sign."

Incompetence in America

63

The Inept Society?

64

Chapter 7: Advised to Leave Seattle

Browne again advises Henry to leave Seattle, but Henry refuses and demands that Frank's death be investigated. Henry says, "Browne look, I can't leave town. The Seattle Police Department has told me not to leave town. Plus this gives me a good chance to be involved in solving Franks's murder.

Browne reluctantly reveals that Frank had been stealing drugs and selling it on the black market modified so much that many users died.

Browne says, "Frank may be with some high level agency within the U.S. Government, but he is also a crook. He has someone who works in a medical facility steal drugs for him, especially opioids, then he repackages them modifying them in the process."

Browne continues talk and says, "Let me show you the reports that our office has received." The reports showed that 1000 pills of 30 mg hydrocodone had been lifted or stolen from one of the major hospitals in Seattle by an orderly who worked there. He passed them on to Frank who repackaged the pills after modifying them to a strength of about 10 percent, then they were sold to a children's hospital who prescribed them to its cancer patients for pain."

The drugs commanded a very high price and Browne's evidence convinces Henry that Frank was up to no good.

Disillusioned, Henry agrees to leave town since there is no reason to protect Frank and the Seattle Police were not about to take on the FBI.

The local police are not going to be happy to see Henry go either. If word gets out that an FBI agent was suspected of several crimes and got away, it would be very embarrassing for them. Meanwhile they are looking for information on Frank's two friends. What are their names and how do they fit into what's happened so far.

What does Henry know about this and about the death of the medical orderly? Did Frank's friends do it or know about it and then there is the murder of the PA. Did Henry have cause to do him in?

Henry gives all this his consideration, he thinks, "It is going to cause a big row when I leave Seattle but I came here to visit Frank thinking that he could get me into the CIA. I know the FBI is also prestigious . . . and now I find that Frank is involved in criminal activities maybe even murder. I don't want any part of it. It's time to move on."

The LA detective thought, "That FBI guy Henry seems like a straight shooter. I would like to know him better." He picks up a phone and dials the number where Henry is staying at the Torrance Holiday Inn. He gets a computer-generated voice and rather that going through the process of waiting and pushing buttons, he hangs up.

Henry is back in his room and begins packing. He is thinking of the people he met in Los Angeles and thinks of Georgia, "She is going to be the first one I visit tomorrow. She keeps flashing across my memory and I cannot get the image of her nipple moving around in that gown she was wearing out of my mind. I know that we would be good together. I just have to take it slow so she doesn't panic."

Incompetence in America

The Inept Society?

Chapter 8: A Goodbye!

Henry visits Georgia to say good-bye and finds that she also knows of Frank's misdeeds, but that her feelings toward him are unchanged. She says, "I have known that he was up to no good, but I still love him even though he is gone and will continue to do so as long as I can." She then tells Henry that she is to be deported. He says, "Georgia, I can understand your feelings for Frank but he is gone and I am most sorry that you are being deported."

Seeing that nothing is going to happen between them, he departs leaving Georgia, he notices someone watching from a dark doorway and a neighbor's lighted window briefly reveals the person to be Frank who flees, ignoring Henry's calls.

Henry summons Browne, who guesses that Frank has gone to the underground and sewers to escape . "Browne says, "It is more that likely that he has gone underground in Seattle which is easy to do. The old parts of the city used to be at a lower level but after it was destroyed by fire over a hundred years ago, the city streets were raised to their current level, which is about the second floor of most of the old buildings. Connections to the underground sewer make the entry easy and once a person is in, they are able to cover great distances."

Henry thinks to himself, "Frank is alive and the crook is escaping capture by using Seattle's old underground."

Frank is running and thinks, "I have been found out. I know my way around the old part of the city and all I have to do is to find the connections to the sewers and I am out of here." He heads for Pioneer square and descends to the underground. He has to go through several buildings until he finds the Cities modified access points to the sewers. He think, "If only I can get to Georgetown which is only a few miles south of here, it is close to Boeing Field where I can grab a plane to get out of town."

The FBI immediately exhumes Frank's coffin and discovers the body is that of the orderly who stole drugs for Frank. The orderly was reported missing after turning informant. The orderly was not only stealing the hydrocodone but other types of opiates and drugs as well. He was stealing them and being paid only a small fraction of what they were bringing after being modified and repackaged.

Georgia is ecstatic upon finding that Frank is still alive. She thinks, "Oh, I was hoping against hope that my love, Frank, would still be alive and return to me. I so look forward to seeing him and taking him in my arms again."

The Inept Society?

Chapter 9: The Meeting

Frank managed to elude everyone and the next day he calls Henry and they agree to meet. Frank still has a good job with the U. S. Government and he decides that he stands a better position of protecting himself by staying in Seattle rather than running. Frank and Henry agree to meet later that day at Seattle's Ferris wheel.

When they meet, Frank threatens Henry's life but he relents when with the fact that the FBI and the Federal Trade Commission already both know that his death and funeral were faked.

Frank presents a monologue on the insignificance of his victims saying, "The full extent of my stance is amoral. That is, it is neither moral nor immoral."

He again offers a job to Henry that is to be under his alias of Jack Alberson and leaves. Browne asks Henry to help lure Frank out to capture him, and Henry agrees, asking for Georgia's safe conduct out of Seattle in exchange.

However Georgia, still ecstatic over the fact that Frank is alive and remains loyal to Frank. She says, "I would like to leave Seattle but the FBI has me under watch and is ready to deport me plus the fact that I am still loyal to Frank no matter how much evidence is against him and I still, very much, want to see him."

Exasperated, Henry decides to leave town but changes his mind after Browne shows Henry the children who are victims of Frank's modified drugs who are brain-damaged. Henry thinks, "I still like Frank but he did such terrible things to the kids, he is not going to change and needs to be taken out of circulation. He want me to go to work with him operating out of the CIA but I'm very much afraid that it would lead to a life of crime"

Incompetence in America

The Inept Society?

78

Chapter 10: The Prison and After

Henry is no longer a suspect now that the Seattle Police know that Frank is alive. They know that some kind of crime has been committed, but what is it? When Clinton asked Henry where they should meet, Henry thought that the Seattle City Prison would be a good place to meet. Clinton came to the prison to where his client Henry had been incarcerated.

While Cllinton was there, the firm he worked for went bankrupted since the people working for the firm were incompetent. They were not trained properly to bill the clients in a timely manner using their procedures. As a result, Clinton was inside the prison's gate without representation. Thus, his pass to leave was no longer valid and since he no longer had a valid release pass, he was stuck in prison.

It was easy for Henry to get out all he had to do was to show his FBI badge. Henry solves the problem for Clinton suggesting that he assault one of the guards to commit a minor crime that caused him to be officially imprisoned and then, hopefully, released. Things went as planned and he thanks Henry but then gets beaten by the other guards and electrocuted. Henry clears the prison with his badge.

Frank never fully learns that Henry works for the FBI. He assumes that Henry works in some agency like the Federal Trade Commission. Frank still works for the CIA and Henry keeps mum about his job for a number of reasons but in this case, it is because the CIA does not get along with the FBI.

Frank says that he is willing to forget about his encounter with Henry if he is willing to work with him. Henry, still trying to keep the communication flowing tells Frank that he will think about it.

Frank still has to deal with the Seattle Police. They want to know who Franks friends were that with him when he supposedly died. They also want to know who murdered the personal assistant and they were in the middle of an investigation to find out how the orderly died.

The Inept Society?

Chapter 11: The Finale

Several days later, Frank left his meeting with Henry and visits Georgia, who is still loyal to Frank and they had wonderful sex with each other. She warns him that Browne is after him just in time since there is a pounding on the door. He tries to escape through the sewers again, but the FBI are there in force.

Browne is still unable to control his anger and says, "I'm going to get that Frank guy, if it's the last thing I do." Browne descends into the underground, shoots at Frank but misses and almost hits Henry. Browne is remorseful but Henry is safe. Browne shoots at Frank again and badly wounds him. Then Frank drags himself up a ladder to a street grating exit but cannot lift it.

Henry with a revolver, follows Frank, reaches him, but hesitates. Frank looks at him and nods. A shot is heard. In the end, Henry kills Frank and makes sure he is dead by shooting him in the head. Henry is thinking about what happened and ponders the situation thinking, "Frank and I had been close friends since we were little kids, I feel terrible about what I just did, but when I think about the little kids with cancer that were suffering, he just had to be put down." Later, Henry attends Frank's second funeral, at the risk of missing his flight out of Seattle.

Browne witnesses Henry and Frank's encounter and knows of their long friendship and tries to console Henry but there is no helping him. Browne says, "Henry, I know you were childhood friend with that guy and that he was your mentor in some things but he was just plain dirt. You cannot feel sorry for a criminal like him. He was just no good and would eventually drag you down."

Henry waits in the cemetery to speak to Georgia. She approaches him from a distance and walks past, ignoring him. Georgia thinks about Henry going over her memories, "I really had a lot of desire for that bronze Greek God, but he was so intimidating with his size and weight. In addition, there is the fact that I still loved Frank no matter what he was doing. However, for him to kill his childhood friend and mentor there is no excuse. I never want to see Henry again and if I do see him I won't even give him the time of day."

The Inept Society?

Chapter 12: Summary

Is America's society as inept as portrayed by Henry in the story? We have to say "Yes, partially".

Many people working for organizations are adept at what they do, unfortunately however, many people act incompetent in their work.

Why? It may be simply that they have not been properly trained or worse, that they are not capable of being trained for a particular job or are not assigned to the right job to begin with.

Henry found that out and was adept at it. However, in his investigations and in real life he was exposed to people that were often falsely carrying out the work they were trained to do. For example, the people he talked with in the course of his investigations were outwardly incompetent but may have been trained to perform as they did.

In Frank's case, his amoral philosophy affected his decisions making him incompetent.

Doc was a quack that had other interests in mind that caused him to be inept.

Browne was often angry but was able to function properly and was adept at what he did.

Incompetence in America

The Inept Society?

About the Author

Jess Browning is former Director of Global Trade, Transportation and Logistics Studies at the University of Washington in Seattle. He has an MPA Degree from the University of Southern

California and a Ph.D. from the University of Washington in Seattle.

At the local level, he served on the Freight Mobility Roundtable; at the national level, he served on the Transportation Research Board's International Trade and Transportation Committee; and at the International level, he served as a U.S. Delegate to APEC's Transportation Working Group.

In retirement, he helped form a Consortium of eight international universities to do joint research and education in the fields of business, advanced technologies, logistics and marine affairs.

Jess is a former entrepreneur having engaged in manufacturing and global trade. He holds eight patents in environmental and process control equipment.

He believes that economic development takes place at many scales that includes from what takes place on the plant floor to what takes place in various regions of the world. He finds no difficulty in moving from one to the other in order to promote economic development.

Jess is an author of about fifty books and has edited many more. He has also given many talks, lectures and keynote addresses at home and abroad. He is married and lives with his wife near Seattle. They have four daughters, six grandsons, four granddaughters and nine great grandchildren.

The Inept Society?

94

Index

B

boulevard, 41

Boulevard, 41

boy, 60

Boy, 9

brain-damaged, 76

breasts, 37, 51, 59

briefly, 71

bringing, 73

Britain, 10

broadly, 30

bronze, 51, 84

brother, 35

Browne, 36, 42, 53, 61, 65, 66, 71, 75, 76, 83, 84, 88

Browning, 3, 5, 11, 91

Brownings, 9

budget, 20

building, 54

buildings, 72

business, 38, 41, 54, 92

button, 17, 47

by-standers, 60

C

cadaver, 59

cadavers, 59

Caleb, 10

California, 10, 92

Canada, 28

cancer, 66, 84

Captain, 9, 10, 11

capture, 72, 75

care, 19, 38, 44, 55

Caroline, 10

Carrie, 13

cascades, 51

case, 23, 27, 28, 37, 48, 80, 87

cases, 5, 22, 30, 38

cemetery, 84

center, 23, 32

Certificate, 48

level, 21, 27, 65, 72, 92

License, 6

Licenses, 6

life, 31, 75, 76, 87

Life, 10

lift, 83

lifted, 65

lighted, 71

like, 22, 30, 31, 51, 52, 54, 67, 76, 80, 84

likely, 21, 71

like-minded, 30

limit, 18

limitation, 21

limited, 18

line, 18, 22

Linguistic, 11

listed, 60

little, 59, 84

lived, 11, 54

living, 60

local, 48, 66, 92

logistics, 92

Logistics, 9, 91

logo, 20

long, 19, 51, 61, 71, 84

longer, 61, 79

long-term, 19

look, 53, 65, 73

Look, 10

looked, 51

looking, 31, 66

looks, 51, 52, 83

love, 52, 53, 54, 71, 73

Love, 10

loved, 35, 37, 52, 84

lover, 55

lovers, 53

Lovers, 9

loves, 53

low, 21

opioid, 18, 20, 21, 28, 35, 47, 97

Opioid, 42, 97

opioids, 18, 21, 24, 27, 30, 65, 97

Opioids, 28, 29, 97

opium-derived, 29

opportunity, 43

orbs, 51

order, 18, 36, 38, 93

orderly, 23, 32, 61, 66, 73, 81

organization, 17, 21, 23, 27, 28, 29, 30

organizations, 17, 21, 23, 27, 29, 36, 87

Organizations, 27

original, 5

other, 23, 29, 35, 43, 48, 53, 56, 60, 73, 80, 83, 88, 93

otherwise, 30

outlaws, 35

outside, 31

over, 17, 18, 20, 47, 51, 72, 76, 84

overbearing, 36

overlap, 30

overpowering, 37

over-prescribing, 18

overreaction, 37

overseen, 19

over-the-counter, 20

overwhelmed, 53

ovulating, 52

own, 30, 36, 38, 51

Owner, 10

oxycodone, 18, 29

OxyContin, 29

P

PA, 38, 54, 59, 60, 67

pacify, 21

paid, 48, 73

References

---

[1] HHS.gov/Opioids: The Prescription Drug www.hhs.gov/opioids (last visited July 2, 2018).

[2] Food and Drug Administration, https://en.wikipedia.org/w/index.php?title=Food_and_Drug_Administration&oldid=846750373 (last visited July 2, 2018).

[3] The U.S. Federal Trade Commission https://www.ftc.gov/ftc-fda-opioid-warning-letters (last visited July 2, 2018).

[4] Adept, https://en.wikipedia.org/w/index.php?title=Adept&oldid=832368546 (last visited June 29, 2018).

[5] Inept, https://en.wiktionary.org/w/index.php?title=inept&oldid=49574381 (last visited June 29, 2018).

[6] Incompetence, https://en.wikipedia.org/w/index.php?title=Incompetence&oldid=848013656 (last visited June 29, 2018).

[7] Opioid epidemic, https://en.wikipedia.org/w/index.php?title=Opioid_epidemic&oldid=847946325 (last visited July 2, 2018).

[8] Organization, https://en.wikipedia.org/w/index.php?title=Organization&oldid=846347357 (last visited June 29, 2018).

[9] Society, https://en.wikipedia.org/w/index.php?title=Society&oldid=846916814 (last visited June 29, 2018).

[10] Orderly, https://en.wikipedia.org/w/index.php?title=Orderly&oldid=844694621 (last visited July 3, 2018).

137